POEMS ABOUT LOVE

MARIA B. HAYDEN

POEMS ABOUT LOVE

First published in 2019 in the United Kingdom
by Rebus Imprint

copyright © 2019 Maria B Hayden

www.mariabhayden.com

"I wish, as well as everybody else, to be perfectly happy; but, like everybody else, it must be in my own way."

Jane Austen
Sense & Sensibility

For Nicholas,
who taught me it was safe to
love again after pain.

MY POETRY STYLE

What is a poem, some words that may rhyme? Or is it a narrative thought caught in time?

For me, it's a feeling that springs from the page. Plain, simple words to connect and engage. A truthful expression that slips from the tongue, where words can gain life in touching someone.

Thank you for your interest in my work, I genuinely appreciate it.

'POEMS ABOUT LOVE' is a collection of poetry divided into three parts. The beautiful beginnings, the calm and enriched middle and the completely earth-shattering endings.

Each poem is an authentic vision of love through my own eyes. There is nothing particularly extraordinary about my journey. It's probably the same as yours.

I have met someone, fallen in love, stayed a while and had my heart broken many times. These poems are my heart singing its story of love.

Grab a cup of coffee, pull up a chair, it's time for some shared reflection, and I hope you find something that resonates for you.

With love,
Maria

CONTENTS

FOR THE BEGINNINGS

FOR THE IN-BETWEEN

CONTENTS

FOR THE ENDINGS

FOR THE BEGINNINGS

I.
FIRST FLUSH OF LOVE

Sweaty palms,
flushed hot face,
head's a mess,
complete disgrace.
Heart is racing, very quick,
feeling high,
feeling sick.
Crazy thoughts running wild
because
you looked at me
and
smiled.

2.
LEGENDARY LOVE

Every once in a while, when
two destined lovers meet,
they fall madly in love
and cannot be discreet.

Hopeless if they fight it,
their hearts are overcome,
and history books are written
as two lives merge into one.

~ LEGENDARY LOVE ~

Like Lancelet and Guinevere
Romeo and Juliet,
such legendary tales of love
are ones we won't forget.

They speak of love that has no end,
of desire, craving and lust,
that enslaved their hearts,
and robbed their minds
till their bodies turned to dust.

We follow in their footsteps
with a love that's just as strong,
and even when we leave this earth
our love will carry on.

As it's written in the stars
throughout eternity,
the destiny of soulmates is
to love eternally.

3.
LOVE AT FIRST SIGHT

It was serendipity
that brought you here to me.

I see the same surprise
as I look into your eyes.

A connection stirs inside
at the moment our souls collide.

~ LOVE AT FIRST SIGHT ~

That's why I feel so sure
that we've met somewhere
before.

And I realise I was right
to believe in love at first sight.

4.
BOLT FROM THE BLUE

I was happy enough,
content alone,
began to accept
a life on my own.

And then you appeared,
like a bolt from the blue,
to enchant this heart
that belongs to you.

5.
CUPID

Cupid raised her bow
and watched the arrow fly.
It struck my heart at once
and missed the passers-by.

And now there is no stopping
my words from breaking free.
I whisper that 'I love you'
and I pray that you love me.

6.
MY HEART

From the moment I open my eyes
till they close at the end of the day,
I think of you all of the time
and thought perhaps I should say,

'If you feel a little lightheaded,
your body is not quite in zone,
it's because my heart has chosen
to beat right next to your own.'

7.
FOREVER YOURS

My eyes are your prisoner.
My heart is your slave.
I know I will love you
from now till the grave.

FOR THE
IN-BETWEEN

8.
REAL LOVE

Real love is strong,
not fragile or weak.
It's built on the promises
that we speak
and grows with the ones
that we keep.

9.
TRUE LOVE

When we started our journey
this love thing was tough.
I was constantly wondering
'was I enough?'

My poor damaged heart
that greeted you then,
was extremely mistrustful
and suspicious of men.

~ TRUE LOVE ~

I'd kissed a few frogs
and a real toad or two,
each time disappointed
that they were not you.

I'd given up hoping
my Prince would come,
completely convinced
that he'd met someone.

~ TRUE LOVE ~

So, I gave up looking.
A little relieved.
Safe from the dangers
of being deceived.

And then you appeared.
I can scarcely believe
you're still by my side
with no plans to leave.

~ TRUE LOVE ~

It's true what they say
that time heals the past,
and I'm so very grateful
I found you at last.

10.
LOVE CONQUERS ALL

When times are hard
and we've had enough,
we somehow keep going
'though sometimes it's tough.

And only with time
have I come to know,
that real love is something
that takes work to grow.

~ LOVE CONQUERS ALL ~

The challenges come,
as often they do,
without preparation
and out of the blue.

But together we stand,
as divided we fall.
Proving the theory
that love conquers all.

II.
LOVE WINS

No more staring at the phone.
No more guessing if you're home.

No more wondering if you care.
No more wishing I was there.

No more games that people play.
No more praying that you'll stay.

~ LOVE WINS ~

No more worrying you'll leave.
No more sighing. I can breathe.

Finally, my day has come,
you are mine and love has won.

12.
IN YOUR EYES

In your eyes I can see
the reflection of mine,
there's hope and love
unbidden by time.

My heart made a wish
and then it came true,
to find my safe place
and it's here with you.

~ IN YOUR EYES~

Now, as your heart beats
its sure steady drum,
my own is beside it
from this moment on.

13.
TIME

You've captured my heart
and enchanted my soul.
From the moment we met
two halves became whole.

There is no beginning
no middle, no end
and no separation
to comprehend.

~ TIME ~

I cannot imagine
my world without you,
and I thank all the stars
that you feel this way too.

14.
MY BELOVED

For years I searched in vain,
for what I did not know.
A discontented feeling lurked
that just refused to go.

And yet, I seemed to have it all.
Life was good to me.
Friends and loved ones by my
side.
Whatever could it be?

~ MY BELOVED ~

And then one day it came,
a bolt out of the blue.
I'd finally found the missing part.
And baby, it was you.

I sensed it in your eyes,
although at first confused,
A single moment stole my heart
and left me quite bemused.

~ MY BELOVED ~

And from that first encounter on
I ceased to feel alone.
As something deep inside cried
out,
'At last, I have found home.'

FOR THE
ENDINGS

15.
WITHOUT YOU

How can the sun rise?
Why does the moon shine?
Haven't they heard
you're no longer mine?

My heart is now broken,
and shattered with pain,
as waves of emotion
drive me insane.

I pray to forget you.
I wish that I could
erase all those moments
when life felt so good.

But my mind keeps refusing,
it wants you to stay,
like a twisted love movie
that's locked in replay.

~ WITHOUT YOU ~

It's driving me crazy,
out of my mind.
Each moment of love
hits 'play', then 'rewind'.

I'm shackled and chained
in this life without you.
Until there's acceptance
what else can I do.

16.
ADDICTION

I have this addiction
to feeling affliction.
It's a contradiction
and self-inflicting.

I'm feeling precocious.
It's simply atrocious.
A wasteful hypnosis
of pointless emotions.

Our future was forming.
You left without warning.
And, now I am scorning
this process of mourning.

17.
THE CHEATER

Don't think for a minute
that you are now free,
because I found out
that you cheated on me.

When you walk out the door
I'll forget your face.
You don't deserve love,
you complete disgrace.

~ THE CHEATER ~

If you think I will grieve for you
then just think again.
You aren't even worth
a moment of pain.

You think that you've won
but what do you know?
You're fooling yourself
if you think love will grow.

~ THE CHEATER ~

You're a cheater. A liar.
And, I've got news for you.
If you cheated on me,
then, you'll cheat on her too.

And even if somehow
you both make it through,
what's built on a lie
can never be true.

18.
A PASSING RAINBOW

I was stupid to trust you.
I thought you were mine.
I never once doubted you,
not one single time.

But I was a fool
and I didn't know,
your love was illusion.
A passing rainbow.

~ A PASSING RAINBOW ~

And, I'll tell you this,
you creature of pain,
you beast with no heart
who drove me insane.

That I was the sun
and you were the rain.

19.
QUESTIONS

When a heart is broken
a life loses hope.
So, what is the answer,
how do we cope?

Can we forgive?
Can we forget?
or wish in vain
we'd never met?

All pain is valid
in heart and mind.
A manifestation
of love that was blind.

What's to be done?
How do we heal?
Is their salvation?
Is anything real?

~ QUESTIONS ~

Can memories filter?
Can they fade?
Can there be light
hidden in shade?

So many questions
run without end.
The primary one,
can the heart mend?

~ QUESTIONS ~

Only one thing
can win this fight.
It's the shadow of time
that comes before light.

20.
THE BROKEN HEART

Where did our burning passion go?
the love that we once knew.
The secret glances in a crowd
that I once shared with you.

Where did all the laughter go?
Those happy times we shared.
When heartfelt promises were
made.
The days that you still cared.

It truly seems a maddening game
to love with all your heart,
and witness slowly, day by day,
such devotion fall apart.

What was it that I did so wrong?
I fail to comprehend.
And yet, I see, our love has died
and reached the bitter end.

~ THE BROKEN HEART ~

All that's left are angry words
seeking out their blame.
And no more tender words of love
are uttered with my name.

However, did it come to this
when all I do is cry?
So, if you truly want to leave,
then simply say 'goodbye'.

21.
EMOTIONS

Waves of emotions.
A deep sea of pain.
Sadness and longing
to drive me insane.

With poor navigation
we lost our way.
A storm engulfed us
and ripped you away.

And now, I'm a shipwreck,
alone on the shore.
Praying that love
will find me once more.

22.
REJECTION

A heart was broken.
Words unspoken,
and a veil descends
that seldom mends.

It's the ghost of pain
claims new love again.

Where bitter mistrust
rises from dust,
and seeps through
the fragile glue.

~ REJECTION ~

If we hope and pray
that they will stay,
but can't forget past pain.
Then, heartbreak comes again.

But if a heart was broken
and words were spoken.

It validates the pain.
So love may come again.

23.
MOVING ON

It's over now
and time to cry.
No more hello's,
just one goodbye.

I'll ride these feelings
and let them out.
I've been here before.
The living without.

~ MOVING ON ~

I'll yell at the sun
that rises for me,
and I'll cry a river
that runs to the sea.

I'll write a long letter
then throw it away.
There was always something
I wanted to say.

~ MOVING ON~

I'll organise things,
that's what I'll do,
remove everything that
reminds me of you.

You may even see me
out there somewhere,
in an Oscar performance
of 'I don't care'.

~ MOVING ON~

And, I'll keep myself busy,
spend time with friends.
One step at a time
until the pain ends.

PLEASE LEAVE ME A REVIEW

If you like my work
and I hope that you do,
please help me find readers
and leave a review.
It won't take a moment
but let's others see,
there's room in their heart
for a writer like me.

*Amazon reviews can make a huge
difference for non-celebrity writers
like me, because it allows us to be
discovered. So, may I humbly, thank
you in advance for popping onto
Amazon and leaving a review for this
book.*

MORE BOOKS

'POEMS ABOUT LOVE' is book one in 'The Emotional Word' series. If you would like to find out more about other titles and future releases, please join my reader's club at
www. mariabhayden.com.

It really is the only way that I can speak to you directly and I sometimes give away some fun free stuff too.
It's completely free to join and I respect your privacy. You can also unsubscribe at any time.

Thank you.

www.mariahbayden.com

Printed in Great Britain
by Amazon